# SOME MAJOR EVENTS IN WORLD WAR II

## THE EUROPEAN THEATER

**1939** SEPTEMBER—Germany invades Poland; Great Britain, France, Australia, & New Zealand declare war on Germany; Battle of the Atlantic begins. NOVEMBER—Russia invades Finland.

**1940** APRIL—Germany invades Denmark & Norway. MAY—Germany invades Belgium, Luxembourg, & The Netherlands; British forces retreat to Dunkirk and escape to England. JUNE—Italy declares war on Britain & France; France surrenders to Germany. JULY—Battle of Britain begins. SEPTEMBER—Italy invades Egypt; Germany, Italy, & Japan form the Axis countries. OCTOBER—Italy invades Greece. NOVEMBER—Battle of Britain over. DECEMBER—Britain attacks Italy in North Africa.

**1941** JANUARY—Allies take Tobruk. FEBRUARY—Rommel arrives at Tripoli. APRIL—Germany invades Greece & Yugoslavia. JUNE—Allies are in Syria; Germany invades Russia. JULY—Russia joins Allies. AUGUST—Germans capture Kiev. OCTOBER—Germany reaches Moscow. DECEMBER—Germans retreat from Moscow; Japan attacks Pearl Harbor; United States enters war against Axis nations.

**1942** MAY—first British bomber attack on Cologne. JUNE—Germans take Tobruk. SEPTEMBER—Battle of Stalingrad begins. OCTOBER—Battle of El Alamein begins. NOVEMBER—Allies recapture Tobruk; Russians counterattack at Stalingrad.

**1943** JANUARY—Allies take Tripoli. FEBRUARY—German troops at Stalingrad surrender. APRIL—revolt of Warsaw Ghetto Jews begins. MAY—German and Italian resistance in North Africa is over; their troops surrender in Tunisia; Warsaw Ghetto revolt is put down by Germany. JULY—allies invade Sicily; Mussolini put in prison. SEPTEMBER—Allies land in Italy; Italians surrender; Germans occupy Rome; Mussolini rescued by Germany. OCTOBER—Allies capture Naples; Italy declares war on Germany. NOVEMBER—Russians recapture Kiev.

**1944** JANUARY—Allies land at Anzio. JUNE—Rome falls to Allies; Allies land in Normandy (D-Day). JULY—assassination attempt on Hitler fails. AUGUST—Allies land in southern France. SEPTEMBER—Brussels freed. OCTOBER—Athens liberated. DECEMBER—Battle of the Bulge.

**1945** JANUARY—Russians free Warsaw. FEBRUARY—Dresden bombed. APRIL—Americans take Belsen and Buchenwald concentration camps; Russians free Vienna; Russians take over Berlin; Mussolini killed; Hitler commits suicide. MAY—Germany surrenders; Goering captured.

## THE PACIFIC THEATER

**1940** SEPTEMBER—Japan joins Axis nations Germany & Italy.

**1941** APRIL—Russia & Japan sign neutrality pact. DECEMBER—Japanese launch attacks against Pearl Harbor, Hong Kong, the Philippines, & Malaya; United States and Allied nations declare war on Japan; China declares war on Japan, Germany, & Italy; Japan takes over Guam, Wake Island, & Hong Kong; Japan attacks Burma.

**1942** JANUARY—Japan takes over Manila; Japan invades Dutch East Indies. FEBRUARY—Japan takes over Singapore; Battle of the Java Sea. APRIL—Japanese overrun Bataan. MAY—Japan takes Mandalay; Allied forces in Philippines surrender to Japan; Japan takes Corregidor; Battle of the Coral Sea. JUNE—Battle of Midway; Japan occupies Aleutian Islands. AUGUST—United States invades Guadalcanal in the Solomon Islands.

**1943** FEBRUARY—Guadalcanal taken by U.S. Marines. MARCH—Japanese begin to retreat in China. APRIL—Yamamoto shot down by U.S. Air Force. MAY—U.S. troops take Aleutian Islands back from Japan. JUNE—Allied troops land in New Guinea. NOVEMBER—U.S. Marines invade Bougainville & Tarawa.

**1944** FEBRUARY—Truk liberated. JUNE—Saipan attacked by United States. JULY—battle for Guam begins. OCTOBER—U.S. troops invade Philippines; Battle of Leyte Gulf won by Allies.

**1945** JANUARY—Luzon taken; Burma Road won back. MARCH—Iwo Jima freed. APRIL—Okinawa attacked by U.S. troops; President Franklin Roosevelt dies; Harry S. Truman becomes president. JUNE—United States takes Okinawa. AUGUST—atomic bomb dropped on Hiroshima; Russia declares war on Japan; atomic bomb dropped on Nagasaki. SEPTEMBER—Japan surrenders.

# WORLD AT WAR

# Warsaw Ghetto

# WORLD · AT · WAR

# Warsaw Ghetto

By R. Conrad Stein

Consultant:
Professor Robert L. Messer, Ph.D.
Department of History
University of Illinois, Chicago

CHILDRENS PRESS ™

CHICAGO

Adolf Hilter reviewing his victory parade after
the collapse of Warsaw, Poland in 1939.

**Library of Congress Cataloging in
Publication Data**

Stein, R. Conrad.
  Warsaw ghetto.

  (World at war)
  Summary: Recounts life in the Jewish quarter
in Warsaw from 1939 to 1945 when the years of
hunger and privation culminated in the complete
destruction of that ghetto.
  1. Warsaw (Poland)—History—Uprising of
1943—Juvenile literature.  2. Jews—Poland—
Warsaw—Persecutions—Juvenile literature.
[1. Warsaw (Poland)—History—Uprising of
1943.  2. Jews—Poland—Warsaw—Persecutions.  3. World War, 1939–1945—Jews.
4. Poland—History—Occupation, 1939–1945]
I. Title.  II. Series.
DS135.P62W365  1985
940.53'15'0392404384      84-23202
ISBN 0-516-04779-5

FRONTISPIECE:
The Warsaw Ghetto wall

PICTURE CREDITS:
SPERTUS MUSEUM OF JUDAICA: Cover, pages 4,
13, 20, 42, 45, 46
NATIONAL ARCHIVES: Pages 6, 9 (top), 23 (top),
24 (bottom), 39 (bottom), 40 (top), 41
EASTFOTO: Pages 9 (bottom), 10, 11, 12 14
(bottom), 15 (right), 17, 18, 28, 29, 36, 40
(bottom), 43
UPI: Pages 14 (top), 44
YIVO INSTITUTE FOR JEWISH RESEARCH, INC.:
Pages 15 (left), 21, 23 (bottom), 24 (top), 26, 27,
31, 32, 35, 39 (top)

COVER PHOTO:
German soldiers mocking a Warsaw Ghetto Jew

PROJECT EDITOR
Joan Downing

CREATIVE DIRECTOR
Margrit Fiddle

For the people of Warsaw, Poland, the month of September, 1939, was a long nightmare. German armies surrounded their city. Day and night the rumble of artillery shook the ground. Hundreds of war planes buzzed over rooftops releasing their deadly bombs. Finally, by the end of the month, the sounds of battle faded as victorious Germans marched into the Polish capital. The fighting was over, but for the civilians the horror of war had just begun.

All of Warsaw's citizens endured hunger and privation during the long years of German occupation. But the city's Jews suffered a holocaust.

World War II in Europe is sometimes called "the war against the Jews." Hatred of Jewish people was basic to Nazi philosophy. Adolf Hitler and the Nazis rose to power in the 1930s largely because they were able to convince the German people that the Jews were responsible for the misfortunes suffered by Germany after World War I. As the war progressed, Jews in territory occupied by the Nazis were systematically murdered.

In eastern Europe, and especially in Poland, the slaughter of Jews reached appalling proportions. It is estimated that fully 90 percent of all Polish Jews failed to survive World War II. Even German Jews fared better than Polish Jews. But in Poland, small pockets of Jewish people fought back. Their most heroic struggle occurred in the Warsaw Ghetto.

Nazi harrassment, imprisonment, and slaughter of Jews in eastern Europe took its greatest toll in Poland. Above: A German soldier oversees the burning of Jewish property in the marketplace at Myslenice. Below: Jewish children between the ages of two and seventeen were imprisoned in this children's concentration camp in Lodz.

"Jewish Section, Trespassing Forbidden," reads
the sign on the entrance gate to the Warsaw Ghetto.

The grim term *ghetto* dates back to medieval
times. In centuries past, Jews were required to
live in walled sections of many European cities.
Those areas were called ghettos. Though that
practice had ended generations earlier, it was
revived by the conquering Nazis. Jews were
penned into tiny neighborhoods in Polish,
Russian, and Hungarian cities. The largest
Jewish ghetto in occupied Europe existed in
Warsaw.

After the walls were built (right), only a few people were allowed to leave for work or on business in the Polish part of Warsaw. German guards checked all passes (left) at the gateway of the ghetto.

Before the war, Warsaw had the largest Jewish population of any European city. Some 400,000 Jewish people lived there. After the German victory, workers built walls and strung rows of barbed wire around a slum area that measured about a hundred square blocks. All non-Jews were ordered to vacate the section. Warsaw's 400,000 Jews, together with about 100,000 other Jews who lived in the countryside, were then herded into the compound. Thus the Warsaw Ghetto was born.

Half a million Jews from other parts of Warsaw and from the surrounding countryside were driven into the Warsaw Ghetto.

The mass movement of half a million people into such a small enclave was described by a Jewish woman named Tosha Bialer: "Try to picture one-third of a large city's population moving through the streets in an endless stream. . . .Pushcarts were about the only method of conveyance we had, and these were piled high with household goods, furnishing much amusement to the German onlookers who delighted in overturning the carts and seeing us scrambling for our effects. . . .Like cattle we were herded into the corral, and the gate was locked behind us."

For the Jews the ordeal of the Warsaw Ghetto was just beginning.

The people within the ghetto's walls were dependent entirely on the Germans for food. The

"Like cattle we were herded into the corral, and the gate was locked behind us."

Germans gave the ghetto people only bread and potatoes to eat. Often the bread was moldy and the potatoes rancid. Hunger gnawed at everyone's insides. "My belly talks, shouts, and drives me mad," wrote one man. A reporter noted that "hunger, sickness, and want are [the people's] constant companions, and death is the only visitor in their homes."

The winter of 1940–41 was the coldest the people of Warsaw could remember. Yet the German authorities allowed no fuel to be shipped into the ghetto. Lumps of coal became so scarce they were called "black pearls."

During the record-breaking cold winter of 1940–41, the Jews of the ghetto suffered terribly. Ghetto residents, including the elderly, were made to shovel snow in freezing temperatures (above), and many families were forced to live in damp, unheated cellars (below) for lack of sufficient living space in the crowded compound.

This man (left) managed to find a few precious sticks of firewood, but these homeless ghetto children (right) may have been among the thousands who died from illness, exposure, or starvation during the terrible winter of 1940–41.

Families broke up precious articles of furniture and burned them in order to enjoy a few moments of warmth. Many Jews had no coats or warm shoes. In his journal, ghetto leader Emanuel Ringelblum wrote: "The most fearsome sight is that of freezing children [standing] dumbly, weeping in the streets with bare feet, bare knees, and torn clothing."

A typhus epidemic swept the overcrowded ghetto. Thousands of people, already weakened by hunger and the constant cold, died of the disease. Children, especially, succumbed to diseases that their freezing and starving bodies could not ward off. A nurse at a makeshift children's hospital wrote this entry on March 20, 1941: "I am on duty from 3 to 11. It is real hell. Children sick with measles lie two or three in one bed. . . .Shaven heads covered with sores swarm with lice. I have no beds, no linens, no covers, no bedclothes. In the corridor lies a child of five swollen with hunger. The child moves its lips begging for a piece of bread. . . .After a few minutes he utters for the last time the words 'a piece of bread' and falls asleep with the plea for bread on his lips."

These starving Jewish children lived in a ghetto refugee center for orphans.

No one knows how many Jews died that first terrible winter in the Warsaw Ghetto. It is a miracle that so many survived until spring. Certainly the Jewish people's ancient folk wisdom helped them to endure. They kept each other's spirits up with simple phrases: "A Jew lives with hope." "Even when the slaughtering knife is at your throat, don't lose hope."

These old men (above) were sitting outside on an old bedspring to take advantage of the first rays of the weak spring sun. The few streetcars in the ghetto (below) carried the Yellow Star of David, a sign required by the Germans to designate anything Jewish.

And spring finally came to the Warsaw Ghetto.

Warmer weather brought renewed spirit to Warsaw's beleaguered Jews. Vegetable gardens sprang up in backyards and in rubble-strewn streets. Old men sat outside to read their religious books. Polish Jews already had been a singing people, and in the spring of 1942 young girls put new words to old tunes:

> Let's be joyous and tell our jokes,
> We'll hold a wake when Hitler chokes.

Spring triggered a cultural explosion that was astonishing after the bitterness of the winter. Newspapers printed on hand-operated presses circulated in the ghetto. People donated books to form neighborhood libraries. Concerts were given on the streets. Even a few movies were smuggled in from the outside.

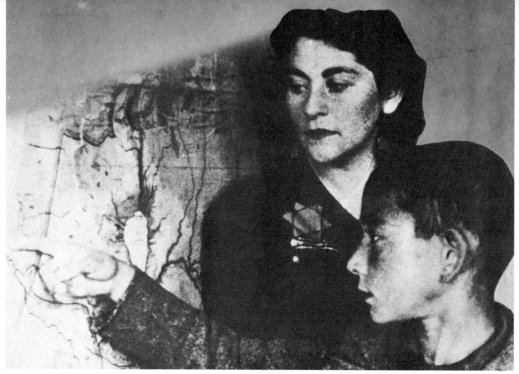
This student and teacher in a secret ghetto classroom were studying Palestine.

The Jews, who had revered scholarship for centuries, set up secret classrooms in basements. Schools were strictly forbidden by the Germans. A teacher named Chaim Kaplan wrote, "Jewish children learn in secret. In time of danger [they] hide their books and notebooks between their trousers and their stomachs, then button their jackets and coats." Another teacher claimed that the pressure of ghetto life actually improved education: "The students went after their studies with zest, wanting to finish in one year a course of two or more years. No more dillydallying, no more excuses. They asked the teachers for more work."

This unlucky child (left) was caught smuggling food. The girl smuggler (right) was sneaking through the barbed wire that surrounded the ghetto before the wall was built.

The gentler spring weather also aided the work of the food smugglers. These smugglers, many of whom were children, became heroes of the ghetto. At night they sneaked through holes in the walls or crawled under barbed wire to get to the streets of greater Warsaw. Many of those discovered by German guards were shot on sight. On the streets the smugglers bought, traded for, or stole food. Then, with sacks bulging with bread and tins of fish, they crept back into the ghetto. A popular song was written to honor them:

> Over the wall, through holes, and past the
>     guard,
> Through the wires, ruins, and fence,
> Plucky, hungry, and determined,
> I sneak through, dart like a cat.

The Germans allowed a form of self-government in the ghetto. A government body called the Judenrat regulated community affairs. The Judenrat was made up of local Jewish leaders. Jewish police, appointed by the Judenrat, patrolled the streets. Both the police force and the Judenrat were hated by most ghetto people because it was said they were mere stooges for the Germans.

The Jewish police (above left) and the Judenrat (below) were hated by most ghetto people because it was said they were mere stooges for the Germans.

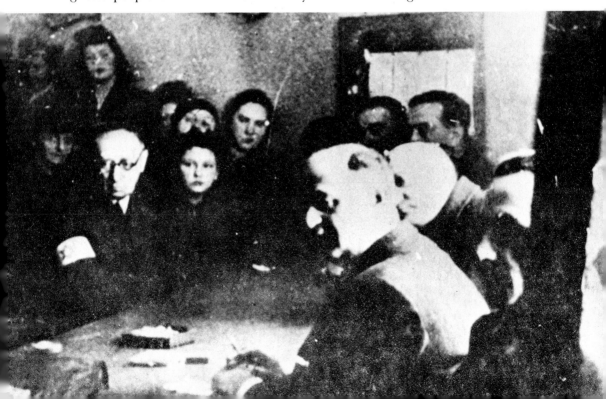

Under the guns of German soldiers (below), thousands of Jews were marched
out of the ghetto to deportation points where they were put on
trains (above) bound for what the Germans said were work camps in the east.

While those in the ghetto enjoyed the spring warmth, secret meetings were being held in Germany. The Nazis had tried to starve the Jews of eastern Europe to death, but the people had managed to survive. So the Nazi leadership devised new plans.

In the Warsaw Ghetto, German overlords announced the start of a "resettlement" program. The Jews were told that large numbers of them were to be transferred to work camps in the east. One of the largest of the camps was at the Polish town of Treblinka, a short train ride from Warsaw. The Nazis claimed that those going to the camps would eat well and be put to work in factories and in farmers' fields.

Starting in July, each day five thousand people were marched through the streets toward the train station. The Germans gave the deportees a generous supply of food. Each marcher clung to three loaves of fresh bread and several tins of marmalade presented to him by

This train, being loaded with ghetto Jews, was headed for the death camp at Treblinka.

German guards. This was more food than most ghetto dwellers had seen in months. Many of the Jews who saw their neighbors carrying so much bread volunteered to go to the work camps.

At first, the Judenrat and the Jewish police force selected the people to be shipped east. On the second day of the operation, the ghetto was stunned by the news that Adam Czerniakow, the head of the Judenrat, had committed suicide by

When he realized that Treblinka was a death camp, Judenrat leader Adam Czerniakow (left) committed suicide.

taking poison. Perhaps he had some idea of the true fate of the deportees, for on his desk was found a note saying that "ten thousand more are demanded for tomorrow, and seven thousand each time. . . ."

Rumors leaked into the ghetto that Treblinka was really a death camp, but most Jews refused to listen to such improbable stories. They argued that in the twentieth century no nation would kill people just because of the religion they practiced. Also, Nazi cunning led many Jews to conclude that the work camps were simply places of toil, as the Germans claimed. To give

In the summer of 1942, 300,000 Warsaw Ghetto Jews
were "exterminated" by the Germans.

credence to their lies, the German authorities
sometimes rejected a handful of hungry Jewish
volunteers because they were deemed "unfit to
work."

Then, bit by bit, shocking and unbelievable
news came to Warsaw through the secret
network of messengers that connected the ghettos
of Poland. Treblinka was not a work camp at
all. It was instead a death station. The rumors
were grimly confirmed. Resettlement meant
death.

By late 1942, there were fewer than a hundred thousand
Jews in the Warsaw Ghetto. These people were among the last to be
"resettled" before the rebels rose against the Germans.

Late in 1942, a small band of ghetto rebels
decided to rise up against the Germans. By that
time, "resettlement," starvation, and disease had
reduced the Warsaw Ghetto's population from
half a million to less than a hundred thousand.
The leaders of the ghetto rebellion were mostly
young, idealistic men and women. They had no
illusions about achieving victory in a military
sense. The rebels wanted only to give some
meaning to their deaths. As one of them wrote in
his diary, "We have nothing to expect but a

choice of two kinds of death. . . .When we fight it will have to be to the last. And to fight means to be killed. . . .In the face of death you can become weak and powerless, or you can become very strong, since there is nothing to lose."

The ghetto fighters needed weapons. Teams of crafty young smugglers were sent into the streets to buy or trade for pistols, bullets, and sticks of dynamite. In basement workshops the rebels fashioned crude bombs from sawed-off water pipes. They sharpened kitchen knives to a fine edge, and made clubs of steel rods.

In January, 1943, the ghetto fighters struck. They deposed the Judenrat and the hated Jewish police force. They proclaimed that the ghetto was now in their hands. At first, the German guards, accustomed to a passive Jewish population, were too astonished to act. Once in power, the rebels distributed leaflets proclaiming, "Jews! Do not resign yourselves to death! Defend yourselves! Grab an axe, an iron bar, or a knife! Let them take you this way if they can."

German troops fighting the Jewish insurgents at the wall.

The original group of rebels numbered only about a thousand young men and women. Yet their actions electrified the community. The great Warsaw Ghetto uprising had begun.

The Nazis refused to believe that a few hotheaded young Jews could defy their authority. So, when the shock wore off, they marched as usual into the walled community seeking their quota of deportees. But they were greeted by the fury of a bold and determined guerrilla force. No

Rebel commander Mordecai Anielewicz (center) is shown among the insurgents in this drawing by a fellow ghetto fighter.

classical warfare with attacks and counterattacks took place within the Warsaw Ghetto. Instead, the Jews waged a bloody, street-by-street, hit-and-run campaign. The ghetto fighters knew every inch of the tangle of gangways and back alleys that sprawled through their compound. They lashed out at the Germans, firing their pistols and hurling their homemade bombs. Then they melted out of sight behind the buildings. Again and again the ghetto fighters struck and disappeared. The Germans were bewildered by this type of battle.

The January battles lasted four days. The ghetto fighters killed twenty Germans and wounded fifty more. Their own losses were frightful. But, miraculously, the ferocious offensive drove the Nazi guards out of the ghetto. A small band of half-starved Jewish men and women, armed with fewer than 150 dilapidated pistols, had forced the mighty German army to retreat. The news was shouted from rooftop to rooftop! "The rebels beat the Germans!" "We won!" "We won!"

The Jewish victory stunned the Nazis. They feared that the Warsaw rebellion would spread to other ghettos in eastern Europe. For the next three months, the Germans surrounded the Warsaw Ghetto and tried to persuade the rebels to lay down their arms. There were no takers.

Enraged, the Germans called on their army. A ruthless general named Juergen Stroop was given the task of destroying resistance in the ghetto. After the war, Stroop was one of many German generals convicted of war crimes. He was sentenced to death and was hanged on September 8, 1951.

General Stroop's forces at Warsaw numbered more than two thousand. They were backed by tanks, artillery, and flamethrowers. This formidable force gathered at the ghetto walls on the evening of April 18, 1943. It was the day before Passover, one of the holiest of Jewish holidays. Trapped in the ghetto, Jewish families retold the story of the first Passover when the ancient Hebrews fled from Egypt to escape the tyrant pharaoh. In the morning, the Jews of Warsaw would face yet another tyrant, and this time there would be no miraculous escape.

As the sun rose, small patrols of German troops entered the ghetto compound. Tanks and armored cars followed the foot soldiers. The Germans advanced steadily until they reached the rebel headquarters on Mila Street. Suddenly

General Juergen Stroop (right) inspects the German troops that were to take part in destroying the resistance in the Warsaw Ghetto.

a hail of bullets and dozens of homemade bombs rained down upon them. On every rooftop and inside each garret window stood a ghetto fighter firing a pistol or hurling a brick or a homemade bomb. General Stroop ordered his tanks to attack. The ghetto fighters flung flaming, gasoline-filled bottles at the metal monsters. One huge tank burst into flames and two more turned back.

German soldiers walk down a flaming ghetto street.

Initially, the well-equipped Germans suffered dozens of defeats at the hands of the ragtag Jews. "What we have lived through after two days of defense defies description in words," wrote ghetto commander Mordecai Anielewicz. "We must realize that what has happened exceeds our most audacious dreams. . . .I have the feeling that what we have dared is of great significance." But the ghetto fighters were fighting a war that was impossible to win. Inside their compound they had no reserves. No bullet they fired, no crumb they ate, no drop of water they drank could be replaced.

After a week of street fighting, General Stroop switched tactics. He moved up heavy guns and pounded the ghetto with around-the-clock artillery bombardment. Finally, the general ordered flamethrower teams to burn down the ghetto.

Even in the face of flames the Jews refused to give up. Their stubborn resistance astonished General Stroop. In his report to Berlin he wrote: "The Jews stayed in the burning buildings until because of the fear of being burned alive they jumped down from the upper stories. . . .With their bones broken they still tried to crawl across the street into buildings which had not yet been set on fire. . . .Despite the danger of being burned alive the Jews and bandits often preferred to return into the flames rather than risk being caught by us."

A Jewish survivor named Marek Edelman described the peril of moving from street to street in the blazing ghetto: "Flames cling to our smoldering clothes. The pavement melts to a sticky black tar beneath our feet. Broken glass, littering the streets, cuts into our shoes. Our soles burn from the heat of the pavement. One by one we stagger through the conflagration. From house to house, courtyard to courtyard, half choked, a hundred hammers beating in our skulls, burning rafters falling over us, we finally pass the area under fire."

Even though they were trapped in the blazing ghetto, the rebels refused to give up.

When the destruction of the ghetto was complete, all hope was lost for most of the few rebel Jews who remained in hiding. They were forced out of the cellars (above) and ruined buildings (below) in which they had taken refuge. Most were slaughtered on the spot; only thirty were "evacuated" to the death camp at Treblinka.

This rebel fighter was forced to surrender.

No amount of human courage could defy the surging wall of flames or the shells the Germans poured into the ghetto. Ghetto dwellers died by the thousands. When the situation proved hopeless, many Jews surrendered and were sent to Treblinka. A small band of ghetto fighters managed a heroic escape through neck-deep water in the Warsaw sewer system. The ghetto commander, twenty-four-year-old Mordecai Anielewicz, and a few other survivors killed themselves rather than surrender to the Germans.

The destruction of the Tlomaki Synagogue (above) on May 16, 1943 signified to German General Juergen Stroop the final destruction of the Warsaw Ghetto.

On May 16, General Stroop wrote his last daily battle report: "The former Jewish quarter of Warsaw is no longer in existence. The large-scale action was terminated at 2015 hours by blowing up the Warsaw [Tlomaki] Synagogue. . . .Total number of Jews dealt with: 56,065, including both Jews caught and Jews whose extermination can be proved."

These few
survivors of the
Warsaw Ghetto
uprising (above)
were on their
way to Treblinka.
Most of the
Jews dragged out
of their bunkers
were shot on
the spot, though
many were forced
to dig their
own graves
beforehand (left).

"The former Jewish quarter of Warsaw is no longer in existence."

The ghetto uprising was over, and with it the Jewish community of Warsaw died. Once the most Jewish city in Europe, Warsaw now had no significant Jewish element remaining. The Polish capital's Jewish population had either been put to death, imprisoned, or had died in the fighting. The scant few Jews remaining in the city hid in sewers or in the homes of Polish friends.

But the courage of Warsaw's Jews never died. They faced enslavement with dignity and death with bravery. Their spirit and their will to survive can be seen in the words of a schoolgirl

The children of the ghetto faced their desperate situation with hope and courage.

named Martha who wrote a poem during the
first awful winter of the Warsaw Ghetto:

> I must be saving these days
> (I have no money to save)
> I must save health and strength,
> Enough to last me a long while.
> I must save my nerves,
> And my thoughts, and my mind,
> And the fire of my spirit;
> I must be saving of the tears that flow—
> I shall need them for a long, long while.
> I must save endurance these stormy days. . .
>
> These things I lack; of these I must be saving!
> All these, the gifts of God,
> I wish to keep.
> How sad I should be
> If I lost them quickly.

Monument to the heroes of the Warsaw Ghetto Uprising.

# Index

Mr. Stein was born and grew up in Chicago. At eighteen he enlisted in the Marine Corps where he served three years. He was a sergeant at discharge. He later received a B.A. in history from the University of Illinois and an M.F.A. from the University of Guanajuato in Mexico.

Although he served in the Marines, Mr. Stein believes that wars are a dreadful waste of human life. He agrees with a statement once uttered by Benjamin Franklin: "There never was a good war or a bad peace." But wars are all too much a part of human history. Mr. Stein hopes that some day there will be no more wars to write about.